T0193903

THE TENNIS COMMANDMENTS

THE TENNIS COMMANDMENTS

WINNING AT AMATEUR TENNIS AND THE PARALLELS TO WINNING AT LIFE

TJ FAULTZ

THE TENNIS COMMANDMENTS
WINNING AT AMATEUR TENNIS AND THE
PARALLELS TO WINNING AT LIFE

iUniverse books may be ordered through booksellers or by contacting:

iUniverse
1663 Liberty Drive
Bloomington, IN 47403
www.iuniverse.com
1-800-Authors (1-800-288-4677)

Because of the dynamic nature of the Internet, any web addresses or links contained in this book may have changed since publication and may no longer be valid. The views expressed in this work are solely those of the author and do not necessarily reflect the views of the publisher, and the publisher hereby disclaims any responsibility for them.

Any people depicted in stock imagery provided by Getty Images are models, and such images are being used for illustrative purposes only. Certain stock imagery © Getty Images.

ISBN: 978-1-5320-6984-0 (sc)
ISBN: 978-1-5320-6985-7 (e)

Library of Congress Control Number: 2019902580

Print information available on the last page.

iUniverse rev. date: 03/12/2019

CHAPTER 1

IMMERSED IN TENNIS AND LOVE

In the beginning there was amateur tennis. Well, sometime after the beginning, say around the 12th century, according to some historians, there was amateur tennis. Since then it has become clear that the professional game has progressed to 140 mile an hour serves, athleticism well above and beyond what would be considered normal for 99.9 percent of all humans, entourages, strict diet regimens, and branding at the highest levels. Amateur tennis, on the other hand, is a crazy game populated by all kinds of sane and not so sane individuals with differing skill sets, practiced and not so practiced levels of play and unique approaches to the game and all its associated peculiarities.

Life generally has become similar in many ways. There are the haves and the have nots and how we got there and whether the system that promulgated that situation is worthy of change is up for debate. That debate will carry on over time and will likely only end in a nasty revolution. Amateur tennis is one path to escape all the daily tumult and confusion. It allows for a diversion from all the tech, all the media, all the chaos and provides an outstanding outlet for the frustrations, big and small, of everyday life. It also provides some interesting anecdotes worth recounting.

I feel it necessary to state very clearly that while the game of tennis has a long and storied history, I don't pretend to be an expert regarding any aspect of the game or its history, or to have any skill at the game beyond the itinerate 3.5 rating which seems to have permanently attached itself to me like a nasty little tick on a dirty dog. The fact is, however, that over the past number of years, I have become seriously immersed in the game. Immersed to the point where I expend a decent amount of time and energy involved in playing and watching others play the game. I spend substantial amounts of time choosing line - ups for the teams my wife and I are captaining. Also, I am distracted by simply thinking about playing the game and pondering and committing to purchases of shoes, clothes, equipment and other applicable items. In addition, I spend an inordinate amount of time watching the Tennis Channel, viewing on line coaching videos and discussing the game whenever the opportunity arises. Tennis now substitutes very well for any number of bad, harmful or negative activities I could be involved in. Involvement in those other activities would likely lead to more serious repercussions than the smart remarks I get when coming home too long after a match (in my wife and daughter's opinion) and after too many post - match beverages (seriously usually just one or two, at most). So, in that respect you might be able to say I love the game of tennis and due to the relatively positive influence it has on my life, and, due to the fact that my spouse plays as well (that point further lessens her success at using the time I spend on court or after matches as a legitimate weapon against me within the context of any argument), I will continue to play it for as long as my body and mind will allow. I have been lucky enough to find a healthy outlet which allows me to exercise, blow off steam and play for pride, personal improvement, and even compete for some reward or recognition.

But that love of the game and the positive influence it provides doesn't mean I can ignore the fact that the amateur game leads to some very interesting occurrences and interactions with some peculiar and unique individuals. The people who play tennis on an amateur level have their own habits and quirks that are similar and sometimes more interesting than the professionals we all admire. Most all players appreciate winning versus losing, but some take it more seriously than others. I too have contributed some bursts of anger, racquet abuse, weird choices regarding shot selection, incongruous decisions regarding conversational topics, and I have witnessed some craziness on the court from playing partners and competitors over the years. It is not necessarily all wine and roses and it's not necessarily always the stuffy interaction that is portrayed on screen in too many not so well produced and directed movies. I have yet to run into a Biff on the tennis court. I'm sure it's only a matter of time, however. Whenever or wherever people get together to chase and hit the little yellow balls around on clay courts, hard courts, grass courts or carpet courts you can be certain that serious competition and serious frustrations of all sorts happen regardless of the level of play. Rules and regulations apply to all things in life and tennis is no exception. The USTA book on rules titled "Friend At Court 2019" is 228 pages long and covers every possible rule, court and ball dimensions and specifications, scoring, and game scenario imaginable. The much less serious idea behind The Tennis Commandments is to apply some fundamental and tried and true standards to amateur tennis and hopefully those standards carry over and help folks with the everyday trials and tribulations of life as well.

All tennis players approach the game with a different set of goals and a unique attitude toward competition. Personally, I don't care whether it's a "friendly" match in advance of a drink and dinner with buddies or a league match that determines if your team goes to Districts / Regionals / Nationals. Winning is everything right? Well, even if it isn't, you still find yourself mumbling "how in the world did we lose to that couple, those guys, that team," etc. And if you did win, then the conversation turns to, "that team didn't have a snowball's chance in you know where of beating us. We played outstanding tennis and we were fundamentally sound in every aspect of the game. We could have taken the Bryan brothers today! Well, maybe one of the Bryan twins against the two of us." Regardless, the general take - away should be that winning is much sweeter than losing.

The folks that say things like, "we're all just out here to have fun, right?" need to understand that the answer to that statement is, NO, NOT REALLY! That approach is reserved for the true casual tennis player that is not interested in improving their game or becoming a competitor that the opposing team has at least some level of trepidation at having to compete against. I am not in any way impugning the character or attitude of those players that are strictly recreational or casual in their approach to the game of tennis, but at the risk of sounding harsh, I do NOT want them A) in my foxhole, B) on my IRS Audit defense team, C) on my side of the net on a tennis court during a competitive match. You need a playing partner who will cover your butt when you mess up and who will close the deal on floaters and sitting ducks when necessary. Otherwise, it's just all for giggles? Really? Come on.

One absolute that I have noticed is that whenever I lose a match, I don't receive a trophy for simply participating or for having fun. In fact, you get that "nice try, great effort," or "that guy makes everybody look like an idiot when he plays them." Oh, really, thanks a lot! That makes me feel better after taking an old - fashioned zero to six, zero to six, woodshedding. Following a pummeling like that I think I would have been better off moving on to pickle ball in my late fifties versus my seventies when it is more socially acceptable and expected at the retirement village. Those beat downs make you wonder why you continue to take lessons, play the friendly's with your buddies and continue to believe that even at a relatively advanced age you can still manage to look like something other than an idiot on the court – hopefully sometimes, every now and again, once in a blue moon, I don't look like an idiot.

That's the thing, every single good shot during a match, and sometimes it really is just a single good shot, throws another ounce more fuel on that little fire that keeps you coming back for more. You know, the return of serve perfectly struck down the alley just past the outstretched racquet of the poacher on the other side; the lob that you somehow manage to track down and after chasing it all the way through the baseline of the court and you manage to muster up enough athleticism to hit a better lob and catch the other guy in no man's land and without a chance to even consider getting a racquet on the ball; or that serve that you miraculously strike exactly the way you intended and paint the T so that the returner doesn't move and can only acknowledge that the shot was "too good." Those are the exhilarating moments.

Then there is the teaching moments and all the thoughts that go through your head before, during and after each point, game, set and match. I know you've heard these and many other thoughts. Next time I will remember to accelerate through the ball and next time I will swing up and out and pronate on my serve and next time I will try not to trip and fall while charging forward for that jerk's drop shot. The pursuit of that drop shot in this case resulted in a stumble bum fall and a right knee "rug burn" that was of concern during the entire balance of the match because I had to expend energy and time performing triage on the bloody mess on my knee. I swear my opponent took some level of weird satisfaction in my situation. I do believe there are still remnants of the clay court below the skin within the scar six months later. Gross, I know. Sad thing is that bloody knee "injury" had very little to do with that double bagel loss in that singles match and the fact that I really spent, like, only 5 minutes nursing the knee during the match makes it not worth discussing in the end. Maybe I should have played it up more and that may have earned some undeserved sympathy or empathy. My opponent sure didn't bother to inquire about it after forcing me to reexamine the idea of taking up tiddlywinks and never, ever playing tennis again. But, who knows, if that had not happened in the first game maybe I could have won 4 or 3, er.....ok, one game? There may be an alternate lesson there, boil your opponent or opponents down to simply another competitor who deserves no sympathy or empathy whatsoever. They only deserve to be dispatched to the ash heap of amateur tennis history as quickly and efficiently as possible. That way you can pound them into the clay without a second of concern regarding their mental or physical health. Seems harsh I know but it might be the path of least resistance on your course to tennis nirvana – playing at your highest level of competition and those dorks on the other side of the net be damned!

Point is, physical love has nothing to do with it. No offense to Tina Turner and "What's Love Got to Do with It" in 1993[1]! When was the last time you saw a marriage proposal on a tennis court? Surely no one has ever gotten married on a tennis court? History seems to indicate that the use of love in tennis' scoring system is believed to have originated along with the game, or some derivation thereof, in roughly the 12 century and from the French word l'oeuf (which in French means, the egg) and could very logically signify nothing or zero. From there the scoring system might be tied to a clock face that was near the original courts in France in medieval times (makes sense given the frustration levels that tennis can create because they sure knew how to torture in medieval times and why not make a game of it, or at least pattern the game's scoring system after the timing used to calculate the tax cheatin' peasant's time on the rack, eh?). As you progress through points, the 15, 30 might have related to seconds and then it is thought they possibly wanted to conclude each game ideally within a confined window of time and therefore the reduction to intervals of 10 going forward (40-30, ad in / out, etc.). The idea being that as the score narrows each game more quickly accelerates to an end.

Regardless of the uniqueness of the scoring system in the game of tennis, there is no love (other than l'oeuf) in tennis. But if played

---

[1] Tina Turner, "What's Love Got to Do With It", Parlophone, 1993

with proper intent and intensity, tennis is war, and there is no love in war, right? Therefore, there is no love in either tennis, or war. But that doesn't mean you can't fall in love with tennis. It's a little like relationships, dating and marriage. You never know what might happen.

CHAPTER 2

NO FALSE IDOLS AND NO EXCUSES!

This should go without saying right? Not so fast. The following list is just a sampling of the "justifications" that I have heard after beating someone (or even after getting beaten up myself) on the tennis court. Commentary added as well.

"I haven't played in weeks!" (Yeah, right.)

"My eyesight has been bothering me – allergies, glaucoma, pink eye, lack of sleep." (Everyone goes through a gradual decline over time regarding their vision. Only Superman avoided that reality. Getting old, if you're not a superhero, stinks on clay.)

"The lights on these courts are horrendous. I had a really hard time tracking the ball." (Everybody is playing on the same court, am I right?)

"The pollen in this town is ridiculous. Watery eyes, runny nose, sinus congestion. I just couldn't play well given the conditions." (I believe I have used this excuse before and received decent levels of sympathy. Not enough sympathy to change the outcome of the match however. Here's a good response – "Just so you know, they make these things called Allergy tablets and they can help." Or, "you know this town is at the top of the list for allergy concerns. How long have you lived here again? Is this your first time on court in decades?")

"I just had my knee replaced six months ago, and I'm just now getting back into tennis. So, you know….." (Oh? What do I know? If you're on the court, then some physician with years of training gave you the ok to participate, right? And you likely ruined your knee playing too much tennis prior to the injury and therefore you are probably better (less incapacitated) than you look with the knee brace and all. So, get over it and move on. Also, that bionic knee is 10 X better than either of my old beater knees, so suck it up).

"I'm so hung over from last night that I didn't play well." (This is a good general excuse and one I used regularly in my younger days. Still didn't change the outcome of any match one way or another. By the way, my sponsor says I shouldn't have referenced those nights too often even though honesty is the best policy and helps on the road to recovery).

"It was too cold."

"New racket."

"It was too hot."

"New glasses."

"The humidity was too high."

"New elbow, hip, shoulder, wrist, etc." (Robots are taking over the world.)

"It drizzled during the tie-breaker and that really threw me off." (Blame the Weather Channel!)

"I just got these shoes and they don't fit properly so I couldn't move well on the court." (No Accountabullfrog Tennis sticker for you! See Chapter 8)

"If that person over there is a 3.5 then I'm a hobby horse." (This is my go-to. Used with impunity whenever I wish, and regarding whatever the applicable level of the match is supposed to be and / or whatever supposed level the applicable player is – 3.0, 3.5, 4.0, etc.)

"This was our first time playing together." (This is used by both winners and losers. When used by winners it is a serious rubbing of the nose in it, and the statement should be taken as offensive language). Charge the net with rackets at the ready!

And if my wife and I have won and the losers trot out some lame excuse as to why they lost, my wife will often say something like, "Oh yeah, well I just came out of a coma. So, you should have won given my condition!" In other words, no sympathy and not to be repetitive, but, NO EXCUSES!

When a statement like "this was our first time playing together" is trotted out by unfortunate losers it is supposed to abrogate responsibility and goes against everything this book stands for. It is also intended to alleviate or mitigate the fact that the losers just got schooled and need to go back to the drawing board to figure out how to play with new partners and how to play winning tennis regardless of how familiar or comfortable you are with your partner, the court condition, the lighting, the weather, etc. At this point, my wife will often say, and I quote, "I have to play with my husband and he's a jerk and he yelled at me too often today! But we still whipped your butts. So, get over it!" She says this to me, not the opponents, ok. The reality is that we talk afterwards and say something like, "you know, in hindsight, if I had been quicker witted, or not so concerned about the court condition, the lighting, the weather, etc, I would have said…..".

Obviously, there are numerous other excuses that have been employed to include any number of additional equipment concerns, noise distractions, complacency, stomach and / intestinal distress, general fatigue (may be a sign of something more serious and should be checked), pharmaceutical side effects (don't load up on meds prior to any serious or even semi-serious athletic endeavor, and especially not prior to operating heavy equipment), hangovers, etc.

Excuses are utilized every day in life as well as before (yes, before sometimes), during, or after tennis matches everywhere with the idea of abrogating responsibility. Even the superstars come up with reasons for poor performances that spark incredulity at times. It really is better to just stand up, admit the errors or that the competitor performed better on that given day and move on. Achievement is born out of failure and the resultant effort to improve on the areas in question and perform better next time. Otherwise, tennis coaches would be out of work and tennis resorts everywhere would be ghost towns.

CHAPTER 3

SHUT YOUR MOUTH AND PITY THE RACQUET (SEE FRONT COVER)

Ok, so I hit a ball in frustration the other day that was originally intended for the net but flew too high and nearly hit my opponent in the back, on the other side of the net. Fortunately, this was just a friendly match and the gentleman accepted my profuse apologies. In a real match this act may have initiated a brawl and would not have reflected well on me, my team, or my club. I need to learn how to reign in this kind of action and along with that determine how to limit the abusive language as well.

This is completely different from the trash talk which was reviewed earlier. Abusive language typically results from frustration, anger, self – pity, immaturity, general lack of self-control, stupidity and / or ignorance. Whatever the reason, it is very rare that abusive language results in any positive change in level of play or the outcome of the game or match. I can't recall any player I have personally encountered cursing and verbally abusing someone and then going on to win the match he or she was playing in at the time. There are pros that have the reputation of achieving greatness with a little helpful abuse now and then but on the amateur level it is surprisingly controlled and rare for these antics to appear. It's a lot like vehicular traffic. I am always amazed that an auto accident doesn't occur every five seconds on every road way in every city, town, state and country. I drive a lot, and OH, the things I've seen!

The reality of the situation is that it all ties back to accountability. Tennis is a game that is controlled by you, yourself in singles. In doubles, you do have to rely on your partner and the moment you start abusing them, I would venture that your chances of winning anything other than the inevitable butt head award are slim to none. Therefore, self-control is invaluable when on court and afterwards. Even when the opponent starts the match with this line, "Which side do you two ladies wish to defend?" Now, that would be ok if it was in fact a ladies' doubles match. In this case it was a match between two guys on my team and two other guys. Those are strong words, especially before the first serve has been struck. It went on from there to include further and even more direct name calling, clear violations of the honor system regarding line calls, lame intimidation tactics and yes, even hitting balls at opposing players. This was not a friendly match and not a cool way to go about any kind of sports related competition. The abusive team lost, thank goodness, and all was right with the world for at least another day. At least until the next match pops up and the ugly, poor sports of the world rear their nasty heads again in order to make someone else's life miserable rather than just their own. The idea, I believe, really is to simply enjoy some friendly competition where winning matters. Someone needs to send out a memo, maybe the USTA?, stating that bringing one's personal life issues, concerns and problems onto the tennis court and trying to take out all your anger, frustration and just plain nuttiness on the other poor unsuspecting singles player or doubles team just is not cool. Maybe there should be some kind of Rorschach test administered before each match to help reveal who is going to be the weirdo for the day. Once revealed they could enter the onsite scif (Sensitive Compartmented Information Facility) which will be newly required by the USTA and containing whatever necessary resources to include psychiatrists, activities and / or media necessary to help expel demons from humans, like maybe an exorcist or a shaman, and that way the future offender can go and privately vent and / or be exorcized of all their anger in advance of the match. Thereby leaving all that personal baggage in the scif and the match goes on and along swimmingly from that point forward. Without this release, the other law - abiding citizen players are often subjected to different forms and levels of abuse and they only wanted to play some tennis, right? If we can't get along on a tennis court then we may all in fact be doomed.

The fortunate thing about tennis is that there is a tool that is readily available for those moments when you get up to your elbows in the frustration alligators. It's the racquet. Sure, you paid good money for the racquet, but they are like golf clubs, they become outmoded annually (it's called planned obsolescence) and you can always drop another $200 or more down the tennis equipment rat hole on-line and / or at the local pro shop. It really is too easy to spend a small fortune on the equipment and then to use the stuff as an outlet valve for the inevitable meltdowns. Just the other day I became frustrated with the state of my game and proceeded to toss my racquet from the service line to the fence at the back of the court. I walked to the racquet, picked it up and threw it into the fence on the other side of the court, I walked to it again, kicked it, and picked it up and threw it at the same fence again. The guys I was playing with were chuckling watching this display. It was juvenile as all get out, but they were very impressed and admiring the fact that I managed (not consciously) to avoid the main support posts for the fence and therefore pretty much kept my racquet intact enough to continue to use it and to fight another day. The fight is usually internal and with my composure and the racquet really has no fault. Regardless, the racquet is the most readily available item with which one can quickly and easily vent the frustration and anger before (yikes), during (sometimes understandable), and after a tough tennis match (still juvenile).

"Tough" is a stretch and is relative, because when I'm not playing well it typically is the obvious result of poor footwork, poor shot preparation, poor court positioning, poor focus and / or too little discipline. Regardless, the poor inanimate racquet is wholly blameless. Oh yeah, tell that to that raging anger within, when it all boils over after the botched overhead! It is just a tennis game, right? No, WINNING IS EVERYTHING! HAVEN'T YOU BEEN LISTENING?!

Ok, here's the real story, and the real lesson to be learned, contained in the following quote by Olympic Champion Wilma Rudolph:

"Winning is great, sure, but if you are really going to do something in life, the secret is learning how to lose. Nobody goes undefeated all the time. If you can pick up after a crushing defeat, and go on to win again, you are going to be a champion someday."[2]

That makes a heck of a lot of sense. But it doesn't lend itself well to the fundamental idea behind this book. Therefore, I'll stick with the winning is everything idea. Until I lose, which will be soon, and then I will have to use Wilma's advice and pick myself up and go back to practicing, taking lessons and put in the hard work which will hopefully help me win again. Translate that to life generally and you will achieve great things. Well, maybe better things than your neighbor or your classmates or your relatives.

---

[2] https://www.thefamouspeople.com, Wilma Rudolph, n.d., accessed12/10/18

CHAPTER 4

HOW AND WHEN TO COMPETE (AKA, THE MENTAL GAME AND SUNDAYS)

Please realize that as soon as the other guy or woman, says anything even remotely close to what I am about to recount, do your best not to listen to anything they say from that point forward. They are simply messing with you psychologically with the intent of getting in your head and if things go their way, you won't be able to tie your shoes by the time the match is over.

Here's the line I heard the other day, immediately following the spin of the racket (which we lost) to determine who would serve first and which side of the court our opponents would defend. Again, I am quoting here, "We will serve. We need all the help we can get playing against you two big hitters." In this case, the two "big hitters" went on to flail, hack, and wail their way to a straight set loss. Wow, flattery will get you everywhere. Including the ability to live rent free right inside my head!

Ok, so this isn't a prize fight. Tennis is a little more refined, right? There is no build up to the match within which the opponents have news conferences where they each weigh in and then they stand within a gnats-eyelash of each other, naked to their briefs (not legal briefs mind you) and breathing each other's oxygen, staring each other down, and eventually the whole charade devolves into a street fight and somebody's mother who was standing idly by ends up in the hospital due to receipt of a professional strength right cross that sorely missed its' mark. Good thing Ma had her wig strapped down because if not, that punch would have taken that wig and sent it flying into next week. As it is, only Ma went flying into next week. No, she will survive, but I don't think she will attend another weigh – in for a boxing match / press conference any time soon. Unless her son or daughter is in line to win a championship belt.

Point is, these head game hijinks are a very clear violation of the etiquette and rules of all sporting events – whether it is ping pong, badminton, sack races or wiffle ball (except for professional boxing, and professional wrestling, of course) and it is not proper to start talking trash before the game has even started - is it?

Ok, maybe it really is, or should be, and maybe tennis should not disqualify itself from these efforts. Why should tennis be so different? Maybe trash talk should be allowed and even promoted. I don't know that Jimmy Connors or McEnroe trash talked before matches. I know it happened during and after matches? McEnroe often directed his tirades at the umpires or other applicable officials. Did Lendl trash talk? How's about Tracy Austin? Or Martina? Does Serena trash talk?

Maybe there should be a push to promote psychological trash talk prior to each amateur tennis match. Can you imagine how that would go? Let's see if we can list some of the things that could be said:

Nice shoes. What, are you in the circus?

You do realize that there is a dress code at this club, right?

Hey, just so you know, your partner told me a minute ago that you stink!

Only Rafa can wear head bands.

Black knee socks, really? They would go well with my business suit!

I heard you were playing very, very well lately. I can't wait to see you play today.

Did I hear your partner just say that he / she had a thousand places they would rather be?

Just relax. This will be painless.

Any chance you can hit solely to my forehand / backhand (whichever the case may be)?

I just awoke from a coma.

Are you used to playing on clay? If not, just know that your ball will sit up a little more than usual. Your shoes will get clay in them too. Your ankles get clay stuck to them as well. Clay can really mess up your plumbing at home too. Clean up well after this butt whupping.

What, not strong enough, young enough, nimble enough, quick enough, fit enough to play singles?

I have been traveling all week and hope to be able to give you some decent competition. (This one works for me because I drive all over, sometimes aimlessly, for my paycheck as a salesman and sit on my brains staring at the windshield most days).

I have not played in two months, but I'll try to compete today.

When was the last time you had your racquet restrung? You, it, and your overall game seem a little loose.

The allergies will kill you out here.

Do you have any bug spray? If you do, I could sure use some, the insects are so annoying!

Do you have any sunscreen? If you do, I could sure use some. Sunburn is so annoying!

I didn't bring any water, Ensure, a towel, lip balm, dried fruit, real fruit (remember the bananas!), grip enhancer, new shoe laces, new grip wraps, a dampener, a racket, a hat, sunglasses, change of underwear, dry shirt, dress whites, collared shirt (required at some clubs), tennis balls, a cheering section. Can you help a guy out?

Do you know who I am playing with?

Do you know who you're playing with?

There's a storm coming.

I noticed during warm up that your service toss is a little out of whack. Might want to consider fixing that problem sooner versus later. It can make all the difference between winning and losing on serve.

Don't let these comments impact your game. Just shrug them off or come up with a witty come back for each nasty comment and put the offending player in their place in advance of (or during) the match, whatever the case may be.

All the head games in the world shouldn't alter or obstruct the fundamental pursuit / goal within any competition – giving 100% and hopefully, winning. Winning makes you feel better about yourself, your team, your family, your country, the world generally and your place in it. After all, it is a boost to your confidence when you win and a ding to your armor when you lose. Sure, self-worth and personal character are improved by being a good sport and graciously accepting a loss as a learning experience and working to grow from it but in the end, winning translates immediately to positive feelings about your game, your effort, yourself and your team, and the losing team can suck it!

Cherish every win, give 100% effort, and compete with the idea in mind that winning really is all that matters in sporting events. Savor the little things in tennis and in life. It can't be good for anyone's psyche to lose consistently and then continue the process of improvement to try to offset the feelings that come along with losing. We all need to see positive results from our efforts. I don't agree with the idea that it is alright to lose without any hope of victory going forward.

It would seem to be a natural fact that if you don't get the chance to relish the wins that are a result of the effort and energy that you have put into improvement then you will eventually become disenchanted and possibly give up the game. Don't let that happen. Figure out what partner you need, what level (3,0, 3.5, 4.0, etc.) at which you need to compete, or even where you need to go (club, Captain, individual team, etc) to ensure you get a taste of winning. Even if you're taking on Middle schoolers. Watch out though, there are many exceptional young players these days given the coaching and teaching that's out there. Regardless, winning will ensure that you continue the hard work to improve and build confidence in your game, so you can play for a lifetime.

Also, remember that Sundays are a good day to practice and play the game of tennis. Just don't sacrifice other more important aspects of life for tennis. Especially on Sundays.

Competitors come in all shapes, sizes and forms and sandbaggers are a special lot. They compete on a different level and also for selfish reasons. That tennis player who just schooled you on Saturday, likely got bumped down from 4.0 to 3.5 (also likely challenged their rating so they could move down) and is out there at that level for a reason. He or she prefers winning over losing. The transition from 3.5 to 4.0 is significant and the difference in level of play is often obvious and measurable. Therefore, he or she finds solace in playing at 3.5 because he or she got consistently waxed at 4.0 and didn't appreciate it and it makes sense for him or her to appeal the rating and move back to 3.5 where he or she can enjoy the game versus him or her having the unenviable experience of getting throttled each time on the court. He or she prefers to school you and go home with a feeling of pride in his or her game, his or her partner, himself or herself, his or her family, his or her country, his or her world. Have some sympathy for him or her, ok? And go easy on him or her given the psychology of it all. But continue the process and work to get better and kick his / her butt next time out!

Regardless of all that head game mumbo, jumbo, always remember to give 100% and play and work like crazy to win when you get on the court. Life is short and winning really is better than losing. It's like the difference between a beautiful, sunny day (winning) versus a gray, gloomy, rainy day (losing). Don't listen to anyone who tells you it doesn't matter.

CHAPTER 5

HOW TO DRESS (AND HOW NOT TO DRESS) AND HOW NOT TO EMBARRASS YOURSELF OR YOUR FAMILY

Please see the following photographs regarding dress code. Remember this is one person's opinion and this is still a free country, and everyone is of course free to wear whatever the heck they like on the court, and then possibly out for dinner or drinks afterward, back to work, or back home to the family who may or may not allow them in the house based solely on their attire. Honor yourself and your family. So, try not to overdo it.

PHOTOS HERE OF "APPROPRIATE ATTIRE" AND "INAPPROPRIATE ATTIRE"

"Decent tennis attire"

"Beware the player in the Panama hat. Not so decent tennis attire"

"Ok. Decent tennis attire"

"Yikes. Beach combing lumberjacks should not play tennis. At least not in anything resembling this outfit. Not so decent tennis attire"

CHAPTER 6

WHAT TO HYDRATE WITH (OR NOT), AND DON'T THREATEN LIVES

The least complicated solution to prevent dehydration is regular old water - and that is all good and obviously proven to work over the years and throughout history. However, the beverage industry has come out with some interesting new hydration options. Some people prefer to pull out their very own this, that, or the other designer fluid (flavored water, green juice, coconut water, etc) and show it off like a piece of jewelry. The pros seem to have a multitude of different beverages they consume. Safe to say we would all like to know the secret recipes. Despite the numerous designer beverage options, one fact remains true, that is that during a tennis match (and any athletic endeavor), regardless of the weather conditions, staying hydrated is an absolute necessity. Nobody really gives a dampener with what beverage you choose to do so. Always remember, don't threaten anyone over their choice of beverage.

This is especially true when you are running around a tennis court in 100 degrees of heat. Yes, I admit that I have succumbed to unhealthy dopiness during a match in all different forms of weather. Even in 45 degrees of NO heat. Never ascertained definitively whether the dopiness that day was the result of dehydration or the chilly temperatures, but I am reminded to ask that captain why we played in those temperatures in the first place. I believe the captain felt it very important (rightfully so, I guess, in this case) to complete the season regardless of threat of frozen fingers, toes, feet, snot on balls and racquets, and general overall frostbite. He was doing the opposing team's captain a solid by allowing them the opportunity to kick our butt and finish their division leading season in less than ideal conditions. They were good enough that the weather played no real role in our loss. We didn't stand a chance in a dome, in a dessert, or in August in Texas. The accommodating captain earned considerable brownie points (within the esteemed "League of Captaincy") for going above and beyond to allow the opponent to complete their superior season. Yeh for them. I'm still recovering from frostbite on 4 toes and one finger. One guess which finger! There were no threats of bodily injury or anything of the sort.

Regardless of the make or model of your preferred fluids, they do help to ensure that you don't fall into a stumbling stupor while you are on court. That can be somewhat embarrassing. There have been times when I staggered around the court and looked like I had decided to hydrate with straight moonshine! Other times when I have witnessed my doubles partner fall into a zombie like state and be of absolutely no assistance at all versus the competition on the other side of the net. That's fun. Fortunately, on that day and in that particular match, my partner recovered enough to assist in eventually winning the match. Mostly because the competition became as dehydrated as we had become, and it turned into a race to get out of the sun, into the shade, drown ourselves in water, and avoid the IV fluid drip at the nearest hospital.

I like Irish whiskey. Irish whiskey is good for all occasions but not necessarily good for hydration purposes before or during a tennis match. Afterward, if you are a responsible adult of legal age, feel free to enjoy and indulge. But obviously not to excess. And don't drive anything or anyone and whatever you do, don't operate heavy machinery! I do recall a USTA match that devolved into the equivalent of a large beer pong game of sorts, on the tennis court with cups of Bourbon versus beer. Our side had lost the match and we were in a mood to try to exact revenge of any sort on the other team and we did it by forcing them to drink more liquor than we did. Not much more, but I do believe we won the "liquor pong" game. As you can imagine, there weren't many direct hits by us amateurs, but the rules were relaxed and eventually anything close was deemed a hit and the point was made and the shot of alcohol was imbibed. The guys who won the original match became more inebriated than we were and in hindsight, I am not sure we won anything that day. Not even revenge for the original loss because we did lose the tennis match and remained soberer (less inebriated) than the competition. In the end it really sounds like just another bad day at the office.

Hydration comes in many forms and food is another avenue for staying in the moment and helping to ensure that you don't get weak, pass out, puke, or start staggering aimlessly during a match. Bananas are a great food product and an exceptional source of potassium and they are a convenient heart healthy, high fiber, energy generating snack to carry on court. Just please be sure to remember that you brought a banana or two along for a match. I can't stress enough not to let them sit in your bag for a few days. The effort to clean an overly ripe and physically abused banana out of your bag after it has fermented for a few days, been smushed by rackets, shoes, sweaty tennis clothes and grungy tennis socks, and incorporated itself in with nasty sweat bands and towels will push you very quickly to find an alternative food product to carry on court the next time around. Not to mention that you will need to procure a new tennis bag. It might just be enough nastiness to make you consider giving up tennis. You will consider deeply, why you decided to bring (and then forget about) the natural, organic fruit as an energy boost during the competition. Try dried banana chips. No fuss, no mush!

Again, there are many options to choose from these days when it comes to "sports food." Energy bars, protein bars, fruit bars, granola bars, all kinds of bars. Personally, I like Irish bars but who's asking? I know, I know, they aren't a good place to hydrate before or during a tennis match. Especially if you are serious about the tennis match. Remember winning is THE ONLY thing – did I say that? Sorry. But seriously, after a tennis match there is nothing like a good Irish bar. Actually, after anything there is nothing like a good Irish bar so if you are a responsible adult of legal age, feel free to imbibe and enjoy some superior adult beverages. Remember don't drink and drive, don't drink and try to play serious tennis and don't drink unless you are a responsible adult and you are at home, have a designated sober transporter from a site other than home or are still capable of standing up and hailing a cab.

Just find a beverage and a food product that travels well and that you can imbibe and eat before, during and after your matches. It doesn't take much so please realize that a full course meal is not realistic. Stick with fruit (safely stowed and easily accessible so you don't forget about it), protein bars (or other bars), nuts, water, preferred sport drink, etc. I usually eat a PB&J a few hours before matches and then bring fruit and a sports drink with me for consumption while playing. Hydrate well the day before and shortly before your matches and that will help avoid cramping and associated ailments.

CHAPTER 7

WHO TO PLAY WITH, WHO TO PLAY AGAINST, AND OVERALL LOYALTY

I played softball for many years and prior to my enlightenment regarding the various competition levels in local softball leagues we would constantly run into the teams (at a "C" level no less) that consisted of the "semi – professional softballers" with their full equipment bags (full of three or four bats, two pairs of shoes, change of shorts / pants, hats, eye black, tobacco (smokeless or straight up cancer sticks), booze, groupy girlfriends / wives and occasionally kids. Yep, they would all pile out of their respective bags and then these guys would proceed to put on a clinic of softballing that would make The King and His Court envious. Thanks to the guy who came up with the home run rule because without that limiting factor these guys would have buried us, embarrassed us, and hammered us into the turf even more than they usually did. What really ticked me off was the smugness with which they typically approached the effort. More often, than not, they would go out of their way to act like it took no effort at all and that frosted my pumpkin. Mostly because it usually didn't take much effort to school us. You see, I'm one of those pain in the butt guys who gives 110% of the 75% worthwhile effort

I have left in this old body while playing any and every sport, or any activity that involves competition. Darts, bowling, golf, tennis, running, whatever. Doesn't matter. If I am going to spend the time, I am going to expend the energy to compete as best I can.

Back to the softballers, we would show up with a dog and a cooler and hope that someone on our squad would bring a bat. Oh, and we brought gloves, most of us did anyway. That humbling experience went on for years until I discovered Church League Softball. What a God send. Pardon the pun but it allowed me to play competitive softball without the threat of getting a metal cleat in the head, a softball hit so hard it embedded in my ear, or the guarantee of losing every game by a 25 to 4 score. I played Church league until I was 50 and was fortunate enough to catch the last out in left field in the final game of the run to that particular Church League Championship. I hung up the cleats after that game. Partly because I witnessed our aged and inflexible pitcher not be able to get up from his kneeling position after the celebratory photo and trophy presentation. He had to be helped up and I understood exactly why. The recovery time from those two a night games and the playoffs had become intolerable.

"I would like to thank my teammates, the coaches, my family, not necessarily in that order for all the good times and resultant good stories." I actually didn't give a formal retirement speech (no one would have listened), except maybe to my family when I got home. That level of softball was an absolute hoot. But it can't go on forever – much like everything else in life. However, tennis can likely be played at different levels forever and ever and then there is Pickleball. So, we got that going for us!

I'll tell you what is not a hoot, this was discussed a little earlier, playing tennis against the self – rated, sand bagging jerks who enjoy the thrill of victory much more than the idea of competing at the appropriate level, taking their lumps and earning the privilege of progressing to the point where he / she earns the victory versus thumping the over- matched competition so that the sand bagger can go to Districts and show off and try to thump everyone there as well. Sour grapes, maybe. But if anything, these folks should be consistently playing up and against better competition. That way they have less chance of hurting any of their opponents and they don't alienate the little people.

These guys seem to rear their ugly heads just when your game is rounding into form and you think you might have figured it out and you might be on your way to progressing from a 3.5 to a 4.0 and you believe each match is winnable and you can't wait to play. (Note: I am not bitter). Then this sand bagger shows up and completely obliterates any dream that you had of hanging with the big boys. It doesn't take much. They return one of your second serves so hard that it takes off the hat of your partner who just barely saved himself from a tennis ball being embedded in his ear (sound familiar), they hit a drop shot that forces you to spin your wheels initially in the effort to move forward to the net only to come up a step or two short by the time the ball has bounced twice. Fortunately, you don't tumble over the net and really embarrass yourself. Only to realize that you pulled two or three different muscles in the effort to determine the true angle to beat the ball to the ground. Then they show their true ability because if and when they do miss their first serve, they serve up this second serve kicker that literally bounces out of the confines of the court on which you are playing and places you in the alley of the court next door where you nearly run into your teammate who is engaged in a raging battle between real 3.5 players that is competitive and fun and an actual test for all involved. You try to get a racquet, or a frame, or a look at the serve as it flies by and make a flailing attempt to return it somewhere in the neighborhood of the opponents' side of the court. No such luck and at that point you are forced to apologize to the teammates and their opponents who are engaged in a seriously competitive match next door (and, again, having fun), for the interruption.

They just look at you and wonder why you felt it necessary to intrude on their match when you should have realized that there was no way on this green earth that you were going to successfully return that serve. You say, "Hey, that was his second! Don't give me that look! He shouldn't be playing in this league or at this level anyway. He's a sandbagger!" Seriously, what really happens is that you simply accept the look, because you would have done the same thing to anybody else that intruded on your match that way, and then you go back to receiving your due punishment at the hands of this over achieving, 4.0 plus player, self-rated ridiculously as a 3.0, and playing in a 3.5 league because he or she doesn't want anyone else to have any fun, EVER! And since you're on the other side of the net from him or her you just bend over and adjust your shoe laces, and like it! Thank you, may I have another.

His or her route to 4.0 / 4.5 glory will be littered with guys like me trying without a tennis ball's chance in you know where, to return his first serve bombs, his second serve kickers, his professional level drop shots, the overly consistent forehand and back hand ground strokes and his thunderous overheads. And there is that smugness again! Good luck and good riddance to him or her as he or she, hopefully, very quickly scales the ladder up the USTA rating system. I don't want to see that guy or woman again unless it's at the doctor's office being treated for plantar fasciitis or tennis elbow, or some such ailment. They should get to experience some pain along the way, right? No, I wouldn't wish that on anyone. Oh, ok, I do wish at least discomfort on people who make the game look uu cuiy at the amateur level. Just a little foot or elbow pain. Not life threatening or anything.

I prefer playing tennis with people who give great effort and strive to improve on each point regardless of the level of competition, the game, set, or match score. They will be rewarded with improvement as they continue this process and they will realize winning as the norm sooner versus later.

CHAPTER 8

ACCOUNTABILITY (ACCOUNTABULLFROG TENNIS) AND INTEGRITY

The discussion turns to accountability. In tennis, as in life, we are all (or all should be in an ideal world) accountable to ourselves and each other. Tennis is a game of accountability. Each player is accountable for his or her play and effort. Obviously, this applies in singles because you are on an island. There is no help, there is no assist, there is no conversation with your partner relative to why this happened and that didn't or why your partner stinks and you don't. Singles shines the light of day on each specific area of your game. There really is no way around being held accountable for every point in singles. For that reason, it can be a very high stress mission to put your game on the line versus the person across the net.

The players that are accomplished at singles are unique athletes in that they can tame the game and maintain their own positive state of mind simultaneously. Doing that while ignoring the fact that the competition is attempting to do the very same thing is a tall order for most people. It truly is a chess match on a larger and more physical scale. Therefore, quality singles players are very valuable within the arena of amateur tennis. Competent singles players can become mercenaries of sorts and "sell" their skills on the open market. They also become more and more rare in the 40+, 55 and over, 65 and above, and so old you fart dust leagues. What is that, Super Senior League? No offense to the elderly. I read of one guy who was still playing in his 90s. You go, old man! I hope to be able to simply get out of bed if I'm fortunate enough (or possibly unfortunate if you ask my family) to reach that age.

Having said that, accountability also plays a major role in doubles tennis. When players are paired together on a doubles team and engaged in a joint effort to defeat the other jerks, sorry, team, on the other side of the net they are accountable to each other for that match and to the rest of their team if it is league competition. In this day, and age, accountability may seem an old fashioned, outdated ideal but it is a necessary old school attribute if you want to succeed on the court. Each point requires team work and coordinated efforts to ensure that you are both communicating properly, moving in tandem properly (think windshield wiper) and putting the other team on the defensive consistently.

One of the keys to winning doubles is to determine the weaknesses of one or both players on the other side of the net and to then act in a manner that allows you to take advantage of those weaknesses which should help ensure victory in the match. If both opposing players are strong and they have relatively few weaknesses than that team will obviously be a very difficult team to beat. However, even the best players have one or two weaknesses and they can be exploited.

If you and or your partner have glaring weaknesses and they are identified early on then it will be a long day on the clay / hardcourt / grass, etc. If you are accountable to your strengths and your court responsibilities, and your team manages to exploit the other team's weaknesses consistently, then you will control the court and the game.

What follows is an informal system for tracking and rewarding your individual accountability in five separate areas of the game. Accountability is key and it is therefore necessary to have an accountability mascot. Accountabullfrog is intentionally goofy but can still be doled out seriously or even not so seriously. Accountabullfrog stickers can be awarded for good play or even poor play depending on how well sarcasm goes over between team mates and within teams. That mascot will be Accountabullfrog (pictured below).

ACCOUNTABULLFROG

Each area of accountability, if performed well during a match can yield an accountabullfrog sticker. The stickers are available at book signings if one is scheduled near you. Fighter pilots (think WWI and WWII) recorded the number of enemy planes they had taken down in air to air combat with stickers near the cockpits of their planes. They may still do that but in these hyper politically correct times I would be surprised if it isn't frowned upon. Regardless, this idea follows suit. Not as serious a situation obviously but the more bullfrogs the better. Strive to achieve as many bullfrogs as possible during each match you play. The idea also ties to the stickers that college football players put on their helmets. Ohio State seems to overdo this, but again, who's counting? Of course, you don't wear a helmet while playing tennis. At least I don't. Not yet anyway. That day may be coming sooner versus later as I age. My wife already wears protective eyewear, so it seems a short step to the helmet for me. That's a whole different business idea in the making.

Regardless, through these five facets of the game, the idea is to obtain the most bullfrog stickers (little stickers – fun eh, ok, maybe goofy but life is too short and why not be a little goofy now and again) possible for each match. Or even just one for a win. The doling out of the stickers can be determined by you, your captain, your partner, whomever. If you are the accountable type and don't mind your racquet or your racquet bag looking like a decorated swag bag from the local zoo as you improve and obtain more stickers, then you can continue to compile a significant number of accountabullfrog stickers. Obviously, everyone will be further intimidated by simply seeing your well decorated accessories even before you step on the court. That may be worth a point or two, right?

These five points of emphasis are up to the individual, team captain, doubles team, etc. If you want to focus on different and / or more or fewer aspects of the game, then feel free. The following list represents the important factors (humble opinion) that should be considered after each match:

1. Serving bullfrog – critique the serve after each match with focus on whether it was controlled well and directed to targets (T serve, body serves or wide serves). Also, calculate how many double faults occurred and whether the ball was consistently put in play to force the opponent to work during their return games. If the service game was generally handled

well and those service games were won in a majority then an Accountabullfrog sticker is available for racquet or bag.

2. Volley bullfrog – were you able to control the net and the games where the points boiled down to your put-away or your ability to transition points from defense to offense for your side? If you handled your net business, then grab an Accountabullfrog sticker.

3. Ground strokes bullfrog – this is more generalized but here there should be a review of efforts regarding forehand, backhand, ("groundies", in other words). If there is a glaring area of weakness that was abused by the opponent during play, then work on that and hold off on accepting a sticker until that segment of the game is improved and the improvements are exhibited in a competitive match.

4. Overhead bullfrog – this stroke can be intimidating for some players to perform but is a very important aspect of controlling play during singles and doubles matches. These shots can make or break a game if the opponent / opponents pop up their return of serve or volleys and the net person is there to definitively end the point with an overhead smash or well directed overhead winner. Also, being able to smoothly take an overhead out of the air and hit it for a winner is a confidence builder for the capable singles player and both members of any doubles team. If this shot was struck with +/- 75% efficiency during the match, then an Accountabullfrog sticker is the reward. Whether winners or losers were hit via overheads can be reserved for higher level players. Those more advanced players don't necessarily need stickers anyway.

5. Movement (court positioning) bullfrog – a very underrated aspect of the game of tennis for the player who is gradually improving is movement and court positioning. This is crucial to review within the context of overall improvement because points can be very easily won and lost due to proper

/ improper court positioning or coordinated movement within a doubles team. There are very subtle movements and then there are very clear cut and well - established rules for movement that fundamentally put a player in a better position to win points. This relates to his or her strengths and, in doubles, to the partner's strengths and how the team moves on court to ensure they are playing to strengths. This is the most effective way to offset the strengths of the opponent. Basically, play the smartest game possible and give 100% effort and play to strengths consistently. If this was performed well during the match under consideration, then take action to acquire an Accountabullfrog sticker.

Once you have acquired enough stickers you can consider an Accountabullfrog t-shirt. Available at a book signing if there ever is one near you. These stickers and t-shirts can be given out for outstanding achievements in life as well. Why not!

CHAPTER 9

LEAGUE OF CAPTAINCY AND SCHEDULE ADHERENCE

So, the USTA regularly goes to the trouble of digitally herding all the cats and arranging a schedule to ensure that league play comes to fruition and that all those participating can enjoy the opportunity to play the sport in a competitive environment. They do this and then prior to the start of the season they make a point to mention the fact that the schedule is the schedule. And certainly, any legitimate changes to the schedule can be negotiated by the respective captains and agreed to be enacted for both teams to suit everyone's best interest. Changes to the original schedule however should only be enacted if there is some ACT OF GOD that demands that a change to the original schedule is necessary.

It is a privilege to play competitive league tennis. There are many people in the world who don't get the opportunity and there are many people in the world with many more serious concerns other than their team's standing in the tennis league of the moment. Those who can participate and who enjoy that privilege should not be overly self-interested and treat it as an opportunity to manipulate the situation to the benefit of their singular interests and at the expense of the general best interest.

Things that warrant a change (ie Acts of God) to the original schedule are hurricanes, earthquakes, floods, thunder storms, hail storms, tornadoes, the apocalypse to include the return of the four horsemen, mud slides, wild fires, rain, snow, sleet, freezing rain, tsunamis, etc.

In most upstanding places, playoffs (Districts, etc) may warrant the opposing captain being forced to make changes to his / her schedule to accommodate the applicable captain who has players participating in said playoffs. Players in playoffs might be close to a legitimate reason to rearrange a scheduled match but still is somewhat questionable. If, as captain, you have players who are good enough to go to the playoffs then hopefully you recognized this in advance and have registered players on your team who are capable of carrying the load while those players are away participating in the playoffs. That would of course be a somewhat stacked team but using playoffs from a previous league as a reasoning for manipulating the original match schedule in an entirely new and different league is somewhat presumptuous at best.

The idea that each captain has the right to manipulate the prescribed schedule to suit his / her needs relative to the availability of his / her best players is a little bogus. The clear cut ideal is that you and your team need to show up at the prescribed and scheduled time for each match with the appropriate number of players and if you don't do that then you forfeit whichever lines for which you don't have representation. Those are the expectations and they are very clear and straightforward and the request to abide by those rules is made at the beginning of every league schedule by the very people who go out of their way to herd the cats and organize the whole kit and caboodle.

Captains are not supposed to consistently change, massage, finagle the schedule to suit their respective players and their respective teams. Putting forth the best and most competitive line up at each match is of course the overriding goal but it is not to be done at the expense of every other team in the league who is trying to adhere to the original dictates of the original schedule. The idea behind the consistent re-scheduling (to include spreading match lines over the course of each week) is to win the league and go to Districts on an annual basis and that is understandable. There is no disagreement that the goal is admirable. However, captains are supposed to arrange their team from the get go to be flexible and talented enough, and most importantly, to be available throughout each league schedule. Then they are supposed to show up at the prescribed dates and times for each match with the appropriate number of players to fill three or five lines (depending on league) and put their best team on the court based on who is available at each date and time. Don't force others (captains and opposing team members) to jump through hoops on your behalf to suit your wants and needs. No manipulation, no excessive antics by the captains before matches or on court during matches. In general, no hijinks overall and everyone will be better off.

It's not hard to imagine that captaining an amateur tennis team is a thankless job. If you look up the saying, herding cats, there might just be a picture of a tennis team captain pulling his or her hair out as a result of pondering the availability, the capability, and the willingness of the players on his or her roster to compete. Captains will inevitably tick someone off by not playing them enough, not pairing them in line with their preferences, not providing alcohol or dancing girls / guys after each match, playing them at Line 3 when they believe they are Line 1 all day, misappropriating league fees to pay for the dancing girls / guys, providing too late notification of re-scheduled match times, not communicating well enough generally, not properly commenting on the results of each match after completion, commenting too much after each match is complete, not sacrificing your own playing time in order to ensure all team members get equal playing time, not challenging opposing captains about the ratings of their players, the condition of the courts, the timing of the make up matches, and not providing appropriate snack food options and beverages (don't forget the Irish Whiskey) during the matches. Oh, and not controlling the weather or providing suitable alternatives to offset foul weather – like overly expensive indoor courts at some posh country club. It's always something. Not much more to be said. Although when you do get that captain that does all the above and more. Buy them a drink (or offer them a banana) after the league play is completed. It is well deserved.

CHAPTER 10

INTERVIEWS WITH REAL, LIVE, AMATEUR TENNIS PLAYERS (NOT TO BE COVETED)

7 Point Interview – George Campbell

TJ: When did you first start playing tennis?

Campbell: In 1976 I played in a Member / Guest at a local club and I was hooked. Managed to make it to Nationals at 4.0 singles in 1985 and finished as runner – up at Sectionals at 4.5 level in 1988, I believe it was. In 1990 I severed my ACL while skiing and it took roughly a year to recover. Unfortunately, I managed to blow out my ACL again at a Member / Guest in January of 1991. I have had two full knee replacements (2014 and 2017) and longtime elbow problems require me to serve underhanded. My son, Geoff Campbell got me back into the game again in 2005.

TJ: What is it about the game that you enjoy the most?

Campbell: I play four times a week, and I love the competition. Playing that often helps to keep me in shape as well. As you know, that one good shot makes your day. Obviously, it can be followed by 5 bad shots but in tennis the good ones come quicker versus golf where you end up waiting another ten minutes to hit the next shot. I often play with my son on weekends and that is very enjoyable too. We have a lot of matches that are very competitive.

TJ: What rating do you have now? Have you progressed up or been bumped down?

Campbell: I am a 3.5 right now and at 72 years young I believe 3.5 is right where I need to be. As I said before I have been as high as 4.5 but that was a few years ago. Spent a decent amount of time at 4.0 but again, 3.5 seems to be a good fit.

TJ: Who is your favorite Professional player?

Campbell: I used to root for Nadal. But I have always liked Federer. His extended career has been impressive and the way he plays seems effortless. He is just fun to watch. I also like Madison Keys although she has lapses in her game on occasion and struggles sometimes against opponents she should easily defeat based on rankings and ability.

TJ: What format do you enjoy most? Singles, doubles, mixed?

Campbell: I played mixed for years but prefer Men's doubles now due to the consistent competition. The pace of play is better all-around because it's faster. Also, the fact that I get to play with my son is enjoyable for me.

TJ: What do you eat / drink before during and after your matches?

Campbell: Afterwards, beer. During a match I drink Gatorade. I am diabetic and therefore I have found that if I don't stay hydrated with water and get some sugar over the course of a match, I will get foggy and lazy. I typically only drink a half bottle of Gatorade during a match and I supplement that with water as well.

TJ: What is your favorite shot in tennis? Are you a baseliner or net warrior?

Campbell: My favorite shot is my backhand volley and therefore I naturally prefer to be up at the net. That's where the fun is and that's where the action is faster paced. As you can imagine, the lob is my nemesis because I am often serving and volleying and forcing play at the net.

George's Game Winning Point: "I owe it all to my son."

Another 7 Point Interview – Catherine DeSouza

TJ: When did you first start playing Tennis? Did you play in High School / College, etc.

DeSouza: I began taking lessons at Battlefield Park Swim & Racquet Club when I was five years old. I used a racquetball racquet. Those were the best days. All of my friends and I would get dropped off at the pool for swim team practice and then we would play tennis. We would get picked up around 5:00. The best days of my childhood. I was playing at Anthem recently and noticed one of my tennis coaches from 1978 was playing on the court next to me. I was so happy to tell him who I was after our matches were over.

TJ: What is it about tennis that you enjoy most? You can discuss doubles versus singles, mixed versus women's, etc. The enjoyment of the competition is a popular theme along with general exercise.

DeSouza: I love the GAME part of tennis - figuring out the puzzle to win or at least keep my opponent out there as long as possible if a win is improbable. Singles and doubles are so enjoyable but very different obviously. Mixed is probably my least favorite because I don't really practice often for mixed matches.

TJ: What rating do you play to now? Have you been bumped up / down during your playing career? Since you are a teacher now where does your rating stand?

DeSouza: I am a 4.0 currently. 3 years ago I was bumped up to 4.0, and i had a terrible year. I wasn't ready and therefore got bumped down. Even though I was a little disappointed, I ended up having an extremely successful year as a 3.5 winning 74 out of 76 matches or something like that. And that didn't even include the WTT and Commonwealth league matches I played. I was on about 20 teams that year. Insane. I don't do that anymore. But, then I was bumped up and have felt very comfortable at the 4.0 level.

TJ: Who is your favorite Pro? Do you root against any of the Pros? I actually like to see Federer lose just because he is too darn good. A lot like Tom Brady and the Patriots.

DeSouza: I have been a Fed fan for a long time. But Sasha Zverev has become one of my faves now. I believe he is the most promising young player out there. I love watching all women play. Especially the young players trying to make it. I am fortunate to be able to see many players compete at the Boar's Head Sports Club twice a year during their Challengers each spring and fall. I would highly recommend visiting there during those weeks. I have seen Frances Tiafoe, Danielle Collins, Jennifer Brady, Dennis Kudla, Noah Ruben and many others.

TJ: Tell me about your favorite particular aspect of the game. Net play, baseline rallies, etc. As a coach, do you tend to focus on certain areas over others?

DeSouza: I really enjoy singles and doubles. I am the most comfortable on the baseline but trying to improve my net game. Mixed is my least favorite only because I don't practice it very much because I play mostly weekday mornings due to my job and family life.

TJ: What do you eat / drink before, during and after matches? I prefer a PBJ before and sometimes (too often), beer afterward.

DeSouza: I have a pretty strict diet including high protein low carbs. Mainly gluten free. It affords me lots of energy. So I eat a light protein meal before a match.

TJ: Please describe your experiences with WTT from the organizational perspective and the amount of work involved. Does coaching compare to that experience or is it less stressful?

DeSouza: I loved coordinating the World TeamTennis and commonwealth leagues for VTA. Being a part of the RVA community tennis scene as well as Charlottesville and Northern Virginia was a wonderful experience. I made so many friends with not only the players but also tennis directors and other tennis pros. It was extremely stressful, but I loved every minute of it. VTA was going through some changes so after my third year, I decided to leave and work full time at Raintree. Currently, I am part of a great team, which makes me really happy. And I am super grateful to Jon Sarosiek of The Boar's Head Sports Club (formerly, he was Director of Tennis at the Wintergreen Tennis Academy) for suggesting I get my certification to teach. Community tennis is important to me and working to grow the game in multiple areas was enjoyable.

Catherine's Game Winning Point: "I have been involved with the Special Olympics Tennis Tournament at the Boar's Head Inn in Charlottesville for three years now. It is a great event which promotes the game on a unique level and it is very important to me as well."

The interviews presented herein provide insight into the type of folks who play amateur tennis and why they love the game. Tennis provides any and everyone with the chance to participate in a sport which allows for continual improvement, the opportunity to play tennis for a lifetime, and the avenue to join a group of people who, for the most part, are active and striving to better themselves relative to the game, refine their sportsmanship and clarify their overall outlook on life. In the end, I would have to say that maybe winning isn't everything, maybe the idea of enjoying the journey of self improvement on and off the tennis court is much more important. Although, in the definitive end, you can probably take that tournament trophy with you into the great beyond, if your family and the funeral home allows.

CHAPTER 11

THE TENNIS COMMANDMENTS

Here's where the fuzzy ball meets the court. Merriam Webster's dictionary defines winning in the following ways.

As a noun

1. The act of one that wins: victory
2. Something won: such as
   a. A captured territory: conquest
   b. Money won by success in a game or competition

As an adjective

1. Of or relating to winning: that wins
   a. The winning ticket
   b. successful especially in competition
2. Tending to please or delight

A winning personality

Obviously winning and losing relates to many things in everyday life. If a person is fortunate enough to win the lottery than winning may be something they no longer have to concern themselves with on an everyday basis. The less compassionate may refer to the "winners and losers in life's lottery." This is an unfortunate description of people's lot in life but can be applied if the idea of offending someone is foreign to the person using the description. On a not so serious level of consideration; amateur tennis is an area where winning can be a difficult proposition to achieve on one's best day. It depends on who that day's partner is, how everyone feels physically and mentally, whether the competition is on their game or not, and of course, if everyone is dressed appropriately, fed and nourished well, and has brought the right attitude to the court.

Ideally, players participate in order to achieve the following goals:

A. Get on the court and enjoy the friendly competition at whatever level of play. And WIN!
B. Practice and work to improve at the game in order to progress up the rating ladder (3.0 to 3.5 to 4.0, etc.). This continued effort should eventually lead to more winning.
C. If progress is achieved and it leads to winning matches as the norm, then the next step can be to work to refine the game to his or her overall satisfaction.

There are many differing opinions, but the game is really very simple from the perspective of why a person would choose to get involved in it in the first place. Sure, it's fun and it can be played until a person is at least 90 years old, and the entire family can enjoy the game and lord knows there are now enough outstanding young, and not so old professionals, to watch that the supply of tennis related entertainment will go on forever. Now, if someone wanted to apply it to their individual overall wellbeing and then to life generally, it prompts a somewhat broader conversation, and everyone can agree to disagree on the following.

There are differing views of history and at the risk of offending some, I intend to borrow from history, tweak one of the original sacred documents from history, and start from the beginning. There was a set of fundamental guide lines laid out many, many ages ago that stated very clearly the rules and regulations that men and women were to live by. Those guide lines were transcribed onto tablets and became known as The Ten Commandments. Obviously over the course of time those fundamental guide lines have been slowly removed from public observance and relegated to very specific venues where they are still promoted, albeit less forcefully and less obviously than in the past. The fundamentals have become watered down and considered less expected and almost voluntary in the modern world. Again, depending on your view, that is either a good thing or a bad thing. We will leave that to others to debate which surely will go on until the end of time. It probably will devolve into a nasty situation as well.

Today, many people still use different sorts of lists as a reference point and as a method for accomplishing goals. Therefore, the following Tennis Commandments apply to both amateur tennis and to life. They are borrowed from the original sacred list mentioned earlier.

1. Have no other interest than tennis. How realistic is this, not very. However, tennis can do this to you. I find that the more a person plays, the more involved in the game they become. This may seem an obvious point, but the game is somewhat demanding and common sense would seem to lead a person to take a break on occasion. Therefore, be certain to temper the obsession. Obviously, make sure it doesn't come before family, work, community, faith and country.

2. Don't idolize any of the game's practitioners beyond reasonable levels. Sure, there are professional stars who

warrant some adoration, but they too are human, they have their racquets strung just like everyone else. Their human flaws may surprise their acolytes in the end. Getting too wrapped up in their success or failure is not healthy. In other words, don't be caught on screen crying at the US Open when Roger Federer loses in the fourth round. Generally, don't idolize celebrities, athletes or anyone to extreme levels. Spouses, significant others, and children are typically more deserving than a tennis star who you really don't know from Adam. All humans, including all tennis players, are imperfect.

3. Try not to curse while on court. This is difficult because there are always going to be those points or games while playing which lead to frustration and anger. That is part of the games' attraction, it will teach how to overcome the inevitable failures, learn from them, and quickly recover to produce the next winning moment. Learn from this and carry it over to everyday life. Be happier for it and be a person that others enjoy being associated with and spending time with. Even as an opponent on the tennis court.

4. Sunday is a good day to play tennis. Ideally rest should be required from already having played too many times during the week. Make sure to tend to the other priorities (family, work, community, faith and country) either before or after a Sunday match.

5. Honor family. See #4 above. Tend to the other priorities namely family.

6. Don't threaten the lives of anyone else on a tennis court. I have heard stories of this type of intimidation tactic being used and it just doesn't have any place within the context of an amateur sporting event. Not that it has any place anywhere else either. A little needling is fine but getting nasty or threatening physical harm is never a good idea. This only leads to law enforcement officials showing up,

lawyers getting involved, and restraining orders, etc. Not a good path to choose.

7.   Be as loyal as you can be to teammates, doubles partners, tennis clubs, etc. There will certainly be times and reasons to switch clubs and partner allegiances over the years but don't forget your point of origin and don't disparage those that allowed the opportunity for more play, contributed to improvement, and accelerated the overall enjoyment of the game. Strong loyalty goes a long way toward being considered an accountable person. Always remember that regardless how sour the relationship becomes between individuals, it takes just one person to initiate a reconciliation.

8.   Play the game with integrity. Don't bend the rules to ensure a specific outcome. That goes against everything the game stands for on the amateur level. One clear example are line calls. They are a matter of individual discernment and they are honor bound. There is no electronic eye making the line calls during the typical amateur tennis match. Golf's rules handle many situations under the individual honor system but in tennis there are few that have a larger impact on the game, set and match. Line calls occur regularly and if anything, they should be a call that sets the stage for friendly competition because they should be consistently generous and not unforgiving. Also, there is room within the rules to allow for negotiation over line calls. If there is uncertainty, defer to partner or competitor and come to a mutual agreement before simply calling the ball one way or the other. If the call is not clear and concise, simply take the time to ensure there is mutual agreement that the call is as correct as possible. This is a good idea in life as well. Talk it out, negotiate in good faith and come to mutually beneficial terms and agreements. Not having to get the lawyers involved will save everyone time, money and the better portion of their mind and soul.

9. We discussed head games, adhering to schedules and the value of being something other than a complete non-conformist previously. Ideally, you get in the competitor's head by playing well enough to overcome their strengths and play as mistake free tennis as possible. Therefore, actual verbal sparring shouldn't be necessary. A little good - natured ribbing is fine but going above and beyond that is completely uncalled for in any amateur sporting event or in life as well. Abiding by the original schedule as prescribed as a team captain makes everyone's life easier. Generally, if you stay inside the white lines and don't constantly crash into, through or over the guardrails then life may just roll along relatively smoothly.

10. Don't covet your opponent's tennis equipment, or his house or yard equipment. Also, whatever you do, don't covet your opponent's mixed doubles tennis partner or his or her life partner either. In other words, ignore the spanking new racquet, shoes, and attire and simply focus on giving 100 percent effort, play your game, and play intelligent tennis regardless of what the competitor brings to the court. Apply this to work, life and relationships and it will undoubtedly make the world a brighter, happier place.

If everyone would abide by these Tennis Commandments going forward then there would likely be peace and harmony throughout all the world, in our time. Regardless of whether tennis is the activity that gets your body, mind and heart going doesn't matter in the larger scheme of things. It really boils down to working every day to be an accountable person who enjoys life and lives it to the fullest measure.

However, tennis can help to keep life in perspective and playing the game, the exercise that goes along with it, and the camaraderie, will very likely help participants maintain a more positive outlook on life. Who knows, maybe you too will learn to love it!

See you on the courts? Game, set, match.

Printed in the United States
By Bookmasters